Language Literacy Lessons

Writing

Intermediate Grades

by Imogene Forte

Incentive Publications, Inc.
Nashville, Tennessee

Illustrated by Gayle S. Harvey
Cover Art by Rebecca Rüegger
Edited by Jean K. Signor

ISBN 0-86530-574-9

PRINTED IN THE UNITED STATES OF AMERICA
www.incentivepublications.com

Table of Contents

Composition And Original Writing 39

HOW TO USE THIS BOOK

Achieving language literacy is a major benchmark in the education of every student in today's classrooms. Without reading, writing, speaking, and listening literacy the process of learning becomes increasingly difficult and the limits placed on academic achievement become more entrenched and solidified each year.

In the information saturated and technology dependent world of today, it is especially important for children to gain and be able to make meaningful use of the skills associated with language literacy at an early age. Success in content-based studies such as Math, Social Studies, and Science, and even in enrichment fields including Art, Music, and Literature are highly dependent on language literacy proficiency. With strong language skills, a student's academic future has fewer bounds and individual goals; expectancies and dreams stand a better chance of being realized. It was with respect for the importance of achieving a high level of language literacy for every student that the Language Literacy Lessons Series was developed.

The purpose of *Language Literacy Lessons: Writing, Intermediate* is to help students achieve the desired literacy milestone through reinforcement of key language skills. The activities in this book have all been designed to provide student practice of essential writing skills. A skills checklist on page 10 details the skills covered. This skills checklist has been carefully gleaned from attention to research related to language, while specific skills associated with each lesson are correlated to the age-appropriate language literacy checklist.

Through the use of the lessons in this book, students will be advancing individual language literacy skills while working toward national standards! For help in lesson planning, an easy-to-use matrix on pages 8 and 9 presents National Language Arts Standards correlations for each lesson in the book.

Not only are the activities correlated to essential literacy skills and National Language Arts Standards, they are imaginative and their open-ended nature will prove to be engaging and of high-interest to students. Student creativity is tapped through intriguing situations to write about, interesting characters to read about, and captivating illustrations to inspire thoughtful student responses.

As language literacy skills improve, increased levels of overall school success will be readily apparent. Language literacy enables students to set achievable goals to go wherever their interests take them and to embark joyfully on a lifelong journey of learning!

STANDARDS MATRIX

STANDARD	ACTIVITY PAGE
Standard 1: Students read a wide range of print and nonprint text to build an understanding of texts, of themselves, and of the cultures of the United States and the world, to acquire new information, to respond to the needs and demands of society and the workplace, and for personal fulfillment. Among these texts are fiction and nonfiction, classic and contemporary works.	27, 51, 53, 74
Standard 2: Students read a wide range of literature from many periods in many genres to build an understanding of the many dimensions (e.g., philosophical, ethical, aesthetic) of human experience.	29, 31, 67, 72, 77
Standard 3: Students apply a wide range of strategies to comprehend, interpret, evaluate, and appreciate texts. They draw on their prior experience, their interactions with other readers and writers, their knowledge of word meaning and of other texts, their identification strategies, and their understanding of textual features (e.g., sound-letter correspondence, sentence structure, context, graphics).	17, 42, 43, 52, 59
Standard 4: Students adjust their use of spoken, written, and visual language (e.g., conventions, style, vocabulary) to communicate effectively with a variety of audiences for a variety of purposes.	13, 14, 15, 30, 56, 63, 76
Standard 5: Students employ a wide range of strategies as they write and use different writing process elements appropriately to communicate with different audiences for a variety of purposes.	16, 26, 46, 61, 66, 71
Standard 6: Students apply knowledge of language structure, language conventions (e.g., spelling and punctuation), media techniques, figurative language, and genre to create, critique, and discuss print and non-print texts.	12, 24, 25, 32

STANDARDS MATRIX

STANDARD	ACTIVITY PAGE
Standard 7: Students conduct research on issues and interests by generating ideas and questions, and by posing problems. They gather, evaluate, and synthesize data from a variety of sources (e.g., print and non-print texts, artifacts, people) to communicate their discoveries in ways that suit their purpose and audience.	18, 21, 34, 45, 50, 65, 70
Standard 8: Students use a variety of technological and informational resources (e.g., libraries, databases, computer networks, video) to gather and synthesize information and to create and communicate knowledge.	20, 36, 37, 38
Standard 9: Students develop an understanding of and respect for diversity in language use, patterns, and dialects across cultures, ethnic groups, geographic regions, and social roles.	35, 48, 54, 60
Standard 10: Students whose first language is not English make use of their first language to develop competency in the English language arts and to develop understanding of content across the curriculum.	22, 49, 58
Standard 11: Students participate as knowledgeable, reflective, creative, and critical members of a variety of literacy communities.	19, 40, 44, 55, 68-69, 75, 78
Standard 12: Students use spoken, written, and visual language to accomplish their own purposes (e.g., for learning, enjoyment, persuasion, and the exchange of information).	28, 33, 41 47, 57, 62 64, 73

SKILLS CHECKLIST

√	SKILL	PAGE
	Recognizing and using nouns	12
	Identifying and using verbs	13
	Identifying and using adjectives	14
	Recognizing and using adverbs to add interest to writing	15
	Identifying and using various parts of speech	16
	Identifying and using antonyms	17
	Identifying and using homonyms	18
	Using descriptive words and phrases	19
	Expanding word knowledge and usage	20, 21
	Spelling	22
	Using quotation marks/finishing a story	25
	Using possessives	26
	Writing conversation/using quotation marks	27, 58
	Using correct punctuation	24, 28, 29
	Using capital letters/writing a letter	30
	Identifying and correcting run-on sentences/punctuation	31
	Writing complete sentences	32, 33
	Identifying and using main idea	34
	Recognizing and using point of view	35
	Writing a paragraph/persuasive writing	36
	Locating and using factual data for writing	37
	Developing writing style	40
	Writing step-by-step directions	41
	Developing plot and sequence	38, 42, 43, 44
	Writing interview questions	45
	Recording interview data	46
	Writing a biography	47
	Writing an autobiography	48
	Descriptive writing	49, 50
	Summarizing	51
	Paraphrasing	52
	Recognizing and writing similes	53
	Writing questions	54
	Word usage/writing a message	55
	Writing a letter	30, 56, 57
	Writing conversation	58
	Writing dialogue	59
	Characterizing/writing sentences	60, 61
	Writing a play	62
	Writing nonsense stories	63
	Writing a tall tale	64
	Developing visual imagery	65
	Writing a cinquain	66
	Writing an acrostic	67
	Writing to express humor	68, 69
	Writing captions for a story/critiquing own writing	70
	Writing an imaginative story	71, 76, 77
	Developing original ideas	72
	Finishing a story	73, 74, 75

Vocabulary Development and Word Usage Skills

Nouns, Nouns, Nouns

A noun is the name of a person, place, or thing.

To review and practice using nouns in a meaningful way, complete each of the activities below.

FOOTBALL

AUTOMOBILE

Fill each of these two baskets with nouns related to the word on the handle.

A proper noun names a particular person, place, or thing.

Fill each of these two baskets with proper nouns.

CALENDAR

SCHOOL

FLOWERS

OCEANS

A plural noun names more than one of something.

Fill each of these two baskets with plural nouns.

Name:

Date:

Nick and Jenny's Story

A verb shows action.

The word-find puzzle below contains the action words left out of Nick and Jenny's Story.

Find and circle the words in the puzzle to complete the sentences.

Then write three sentences or less to give the story a happy or sad ending.

Nick and Jenny's fate is up to you!

On a lovely summer day, Nick and Jenny were _____ by the pool. They knew they should have been inside _____ for this afternoon's big test. Some of their friends _____ by on their way to the library. They were _____ quickly and _____ excitedly about the test. They _____ to Nick and Jenny to come with them. The happy two just _____ lazily and continued to _____ in the sun. "We'll _____ later," Nick said. "I was _____ ," said Jenny. "Maybe we should _____ our notes." "Let's _____ lunch first," Nick said. "The sun is _____ so brightly just now. We'll have time to study after lunch." Jenny _____ the lunch bag and _____ out the sandwiches. Nick _____ the ham and cheese and _____ the chicken to Jenny. Soda, chips, and cookies _____ a perfect picnic. With full stomachs under the bright, warm sun, they both _____ asleep.

S	L	O	U	N	G	I	N	G	P
T	A	L	K	I	N	G	B	T	A
U	X	W	J	H	O	Y	Z	H	S
D	C	A	L	L	E	D	U	I	S
Y	M	L	H	S	I	K	S	N	E
I	J	K	O	J	R	M	T	K	D
N	B	I	P	B	E	X	U	I	S
G	W	N	W	A	V	E	D	N	P
F	E	G	O	S	I	W	Y	G	R
P	A	U	R	K	E	Q	B	T	E
H	T	C	R	H	W	A	K	P	A
M	Q	J	Y	O	P	E	N	E	D
S	H	I	N	I	N	G	W	K	O
G	F	S	E	L	E	C	T	E	D
A	E	B	F	E	L	L	J	B	X
V	C	O	M	P	L	E	T	E	D
E	K	I	C	N	Y	E	N	J	A
Z	T	R	A	W	H	C	S	L	I

WORD LIST
- lounging
- studying
- passed
- walking
- talking
- called
- waved
- bask
- worry
- thinking
- review
- eat
- shining
- study
- opened
- spread
- selected
- gave
- completed
- fell

Your Ending: _____

_____

_____

_____

_____

Name: _____ Date: _____

Identifying and Using Verbs

Sundae Afternoon

Adjectives are used to help readers see a person, place, or thing as the writer sees it.

The writer of the story below used too many adjectives.

Read the story and circle all the adjectives.

Rewrite the story, using fewer adjectives to make the story clearer and more interesting.

As you eliminate the adjectives from the story, write them in the trash can at the bottom of the page.

Pat decided one afternoon to make a big, giant, huge ice cream sundae. He opened the freezer and took out containers of three of his best-liked, favorite flavors. He put two large, oversized scoops of each into a clear, crystal, glass bowl. Then he poured sweet, sugary, syrupy chocolate sauce on top of it. He added billowy, fluffy whipped cream and some little, small pieces of chopped pecan. After topping his sundae with a luscious bright red cherry, Pat was ready to eat. He had created a delicious-looking, scrumptious-tasting sundae, just as he had imagined.

THROW DISCARDED WORDS HERE

Name: _____

Date: _____

Identifying and Using Adjectives

Patience Rewarded

Underline the adverbs in the sentences below.

On the line below each sentence, write an adverb from the word list that can be used in place of each underlined word.

Word List:			
precisely			positively
eagerly	soon	remarkably	apparently
frequently	barely	approximately	partially

1. Andy had seen raccoons often in the woods near his house, and he decided to observe a raccoon for his science project.

   _____

2. He had read that raccoons wash their food, and he knew he absolutely had to see it for himself.

   _____

3. After dinner one evening, Andy took some fruit and corn and walked to a spot roughly fifteen feet inside the woods near a stream.

   _____

4. He placed the food beside the stream and moved behind a tree so he would be partly hidden.

   _____

5. Hopefully, he watched for the raccoon to appear.

   _____

6. He waited for half an hour, but seemingly it wasn't a good night to observe raccoons.

   _____

7. The moon was slowly disappearing behind a cloud.

   _____

8. It was getting dark, and Andy could hardly see.

   _____

9. Promptly, just as he was ready to give up, he heard a sound. It was his raccoon!

   _____

10. Surprisingly, the experiment worked after all!

   _____

Name: _____ Date: _____

Language Literacy Lessons / Writing Intermediate
Copyright ©2002 by Incentive Publications, Inc.
Nashville, TN.

Recognizing and Using Adverbs to Add Interest to Writing

Computer Countdown

Take this quiz to find out if you are a real computer whiz.

Tell the part of speech of each word in the sentences below by writing the proper number from the computer code in each space.

Add up the numbers in each line and compare your total with the "computer total" at the end of each line.

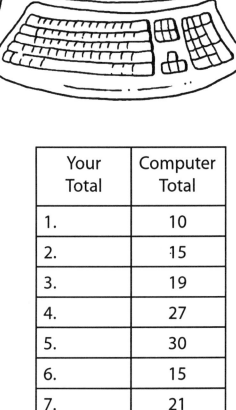

Code: Noun 1
Verb 2
Adjective 3
Adverb 4
Preposition 5
Conjunction 6
Pronoun 7
Interjection 8

	Your Total	Computer Total
1.		10
2.		15
3.		19
4.		27
5.		30
6.		15
7.		21

1. Here is a computer.

__ __ __ __

2. It can provide valuable information.

__ __ __ __ __

3. Have you ever used a computer?

__ __ __ __ __ __

4. Put the plug into the socket and turn the switch.

__ __ __ __ __ __ __ __ __

5. The computer will tell you how to operate it.

__ __ __ __ __ __ __ __

6. Can you read the printout?

__ __ __ __ __

7. Oh! Someone unplugged the computer!

__ __ __ __

  Date:

Identifying and Using Various Parts of Speech

Troll Turnabout

In an old fairy tale, a princess turned a frog back into a prince just by kissing it. See if you can do the same for a poor prince who was turned into a troll by an evil sorcerer.

Read the paragraph below. Turn the troll into a prince by rewriting the paragraph. Use the correct antonym from the antonym tree for every underlined word.

Once there was a very ugly troll. He was squat and dark and had short, dark, straight hair. His clothes were of the coarsest black cotton, and his old sandals were made of straw and were sloppily sewn together. His hand was weak, and he often used his dingy club to do bad deeds. He was very unhappy, for everyone hated him. People disliked him because of his mean nature. He always had cruel things to say, and tried to hurt people in trouble.

tall
long
prince
strong
carefully
good
blond
pleasant
loved
kind
finest
happy
silk
curly
boots
sword
enjoyed
white
new
sparkling
fair
handsome
help
leather

_____

_____

_____

_____

_____

_____

_____

_____

_____

_____

_____

_____

Name: _____   Date: _____

Language Literacy Lessons / Writing Intermediate
Copyright ©2002 by Incentive Publications, Inc.
Nashville, TN.

Identifying and Using Antonyms

Homonym Hunt

A homonym is a word that is pronounced exactly like another word but is often spelled differently, and always has a different meaning.

Find and circle a homonym in the word-find puzzle for each picture.

Language Literacy Lessons / Writing Intermediate
Copyright ©2002 by Incentive Publications, Inc.
Nashville, TN.

Gifts Galore

Many people like to order gifts by mail.

The companies that sell the gifts mail catalogs with pictures and short descriptions of the items. The customers look at the pictures, read the descriptions, and decide which items to buy.

Pretend that you are in charge of writing the descriptions that will convince a customer to buy each of the following items. Be sure the descriptions are brief and will grab the customer's attention.

Magic Kite

Winged Horse

Homework Machine

Fancy Feet Shoelaces

Personalized Pencils

Name: _____

Date: _____

Using Descriptive Language

Stretching Your Word Power

Choose one of the following words.

Then follow the directions for "stretching your word power."

Buy   Night   Fair   New

Look up the meaning in your dictionary.

(word) _____ *(meaning)* _____

_____

Write the words which come before and after this word on the dictionary page.

_____   _____

Write words that rhyme with this word.

_____ _____ _____ _____ _____ _____

Write: Synonyms 1. _____   Antonyms 1. _____

2. _____   2. _____

3. _____   3. _____

Homonym 1. _____

Write new words made from this word by adding prefixes or suffixes.

_____ _____ _____ _____ _____

Write a sentence using the word.

_____

_____

Name: _____   Date: _____

Language Literacy Lessons / Writing Intermediate
Copyright ©2002 by Incentive Publications, Inc.
Nashville, TN.

Vocabulary Vitamins

Do you tend to use the same old words over and over in your speaking and writing? Are you a tiny bit lazy about seeking out and using new words? Or do you just not think about it?

Maybe you need your vocabulary vitamins.

Get started on a vocabulary health improvement plan to zip up your tired vocabulary.

Fill the vitamin bottle below with colorful and exciting words that you do not ordinarily use.

After your bottle is full, take a "dose" by trying to use each word in either speaking or writing within the next three days. Circle each word as you use it.

Name: _____   Date: _____

Expanding Word Knowledge and Usage

Step Up to Better Spelling

Good writers have to be good spellers.

Using the steps below to study new words will help to improve spelling skills.

Read the steps carefully, then copy them on the steps in the order they should be used.

5. Write the word again.

4. Close your eyes. Try to "see" the word as you spell it.

3. Check to see if you spelled it correctly this time. If not, study it again.

2. Cover the word with your hand. Write it. Raise your hand to see if you spelled it correctly. If not, close your eyes and try to "see" it again.

1. Look at the word carefully. Go over each letter.

Technical Writing

Punctuation Rating

Read each punctuation rule carefully.

Use the rating scale to show how often you use each rule.

Add up your points. If your punctuation rating is below 50, study your punctuation rules.

	Always 4	Most of the time 3	Some of the time 2	Almost never 1
I use a period:				
1. at the end of a declarative sentence				
2. after numerals and letters in outlines				
3. at the end of an imperative sentence				
4. after an abbreviation or initial				
I use a question mark:				
5. at the end of an interrogative sentence				
I use an exclamation point:				
6. at the end of an exclamatory sentence				
I use a comma:				
7. to separate items in a series				
8. to separate the day of the month from the year				
9. to separate a direct quotation from the rest of the sentence				
10. after the greeting in a friendly manner				
I use an apostrophe:				
11. to show possession				
12. in contractions				
I use quotation marks:				
13. to enclose the exact words of a speaker				
14. around the titles of short stories, poems, and songs				
TOTALS:				

Name: _____   Date: _____

Using Correct Punctuation

Language Literacy Lessons / Writing Intermediate
Copyright ©2002 by Incentive Publications, Inc.
Nashville, TN.

Punctuation Situation

Read the story below.

First, write in the correct punctuation marks. Then write three sentences to supply a surprise ending.

What would you do if you found yourself on a strange planet and the only sign of life you saw was a rock that had Punctuation Planet written on it Maybe you would look for a trail or footprints I don't know what I would do but one thing I do know is that I would be frightened I would want to find a friend or two or look for a way to send a message back to Earth I would begin to look around for food shelter and clothing just in case no rescue came Can you imagine being in this punctuation situation

Well I _____

_____

_____

_____

_____

_____

_____

_____

Name: _____   Date: _____

Language Literacy Lessons / Writing Intermediate
Copyright ©2002 by Incentive Publications, Inc.
Nashville, TN.

Using Quotation Marks/Finishing a Story

Royal Possessions

On the line under each picture, write a phrase that labels the picture.

Make the first word in each phrase show possession.

Then on the lines below, write a short story using the phrases.

| _____ | _____ | _____ |
| (king, throne) | (queen, crown) | (princess, cloak) |

| _____ | _____ | _____ |
| (dog, fleas) | (beggar, rags) | (watchman, keys) |

_____

_____

_____

_____

_____

_____

_____

_____

Name: _____

Date: _____

Using Possessives

Language Literacy Lessons / Writing Intermediate
Copyright ©2002 by Incentive Publications, Inc.
Nashville, TN.

All Advice is Not Good Advice

Read about the fox and the goat.

Rewrite the story and make up the conversation between the fox and the goat. Use quotation marks around the words when the goat and fox are speaking.

The Fox and the Goat

A fox fell into a well and was unable to escape. He was trying to solve his problem when a thirsty goat came along.

The goat asked if the water was good and whether there was enough for him.

The fox replied that there was plenty of delicious water and invited the goat into the well to quench his thirst.

The goat couldn't resist and leaped into the well. The fox climbed up on the goat's horns and escaped. When he got out, he called down to the trapped goat.

He told the goat that if he had half as much of a brain as he had a beard, he would have looked before he leaped.

_____

_____

_____

_____

_____

_____

_____

_____

_____

_____

Name: _____ Date: _____

Language Literacy Lessons / Writing Intermediate
Copyright ©2002 by Incentive Publications, Inc.
Nashville, TN.

Writing Conversation/Using Quotation Marks

BLACKOUT

Think of 7 items that are powered by electricity that you or members of your family use every day.

Write the name of each item on a line below. Beside each item's name, write a good sentence to tell how you could replace it or substitute for its use if there were an electrical blackout for 30 days. Do not forget to use capital letters and correct punctuation as needed.

1. _____ _____

_____

2. _____ _____

_____

3. _____ _____

_____

4. _____ _____

_____

5. _____ _____

_____

6. _____ _____

_____

7. _____ _____

_____

Language Literacy Lessons / Writing Intermediate
Copyright ©2002 by Incentive Publications, Inc.
Nashville, TN.

Poor Peter

Read poor Peter's story and supply the missing punctuation marks.

Check your work by crossing out each punctuation symbol as you place it correctly in the story.

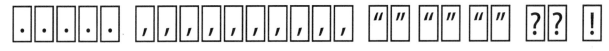

Finish the story.

Peter awoke suddenly and sat up in bed He held his hand over his mouth to smother the scream that he felt was coming His heart beat wildly and he could hardly breathe Where was that strange noise coming from The same thud thud thud then a loud clump was repeated over and over It sounded like a large body coming downstairs 3 at a time resting on the fourth step and starting over Peter knew however that there were no steps inside the house As he crept silently from his bed he thought to himself Why oh why did I insist on staying home alone on Friday the thirteenth

Just then _____

_____

_____

_____

_____

_____

_____

_____

_____

_____

Language Literacy Lessons / Writing Intermediate

Copyright ©2002 by Incentive Publications, Inc.
Nashville, TN.

Using Correct Punctuation/Finishing a Story

Supply the Capitals

Barbara Ann wrote this letter to her friend Jerry. Jerry didn't answer the letter.

Could it have been because Barbara Ann failed to use capital letters in her letter?

Correct the letter by writing the necessary capitals over the lowercase letters. When you have finished, turn the page upside down to find all the letters you should have used.

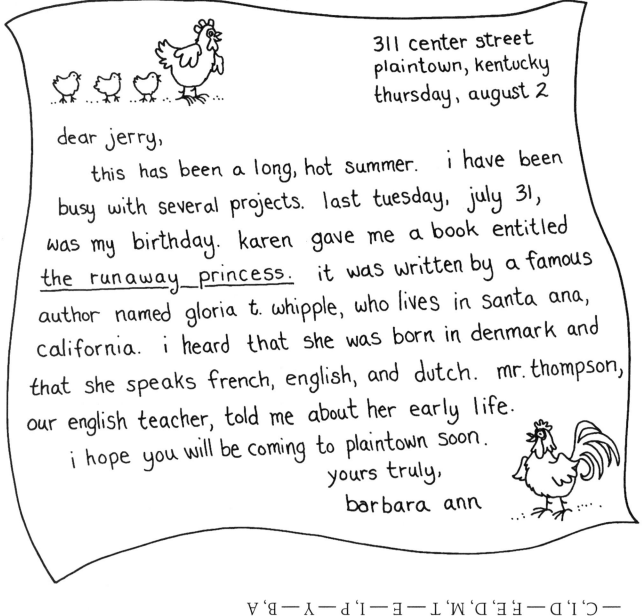

311 center street
plaintown, kentucky
thursday, august 2

dear jerry,

    this has been a long, hot summer. i have been busy with several projects. last tuesday, july 31, was my birthday. karen gave me a book entitled <u>the runaway princess.</u> it was written by a famous author named gloria t. whipple, who lives in santa ana, california. i heard that she was born in denmark and that she speaks french, english, and dutch. mr. thompson, our english teacher, told me about her early life. i hope you will be coming to plaintown soon.

        yours truly,

        barbara ann

C,I,D—F,E,D,M,T—E—I,P—Y—B,A
C,S—P,K—T,A—D,J—T,I—L,T,J—K—T,R,P,I—G,T,W,S,A

Becky's First Visit

The following paragraph contains run-on sentences.

Rewrite the paragraph and divide the sentences that are too long into more readable ones. Make the paragraph flow smoothly.

Check your punctuation to make sure it is correct.

My cousin Becky came to visit for the first time and I wanted to give her the grand tour of my neighborhood so she could meet all my friends. We walked up and down the block and I introduced her to some people and said that we would all play together after dinner. Then I took out some of my allowance and said I would treat Becky to an ice cream cone but she preferred a Popsicle instead. We arrived home in time for dinner but neither of us was hungry and we stared at our food. We sat for an hour and we couldn't eat but all the other kids were back outside and they were choosing teams for a kickball game. We were wishing that we had waited until after dinner for dessert but it was too late to worry about a decision we had made in haste and without thinking about the consequences. It looked as if another day might pass before Becky got to play with my friends.

_____

_____

_____

_____

_____

_____

_____

_____

_____

_____

Name: _____   Date: _____

Language Literacy Lessons / Writing Intermediate
Copyright ©2002 by Incentive Publications, Inc.
Nashville, TN.

Identifying And Correcting Run-On Sentences/Punctuation

Sprout A Thought

A sentence expresses a complete thought and should always make sense.

Read the sentences and phrases below.

If the words form a sentence, place the correct punctuation mark at the end. Use your pencil to shade in the spaces in the puzzle that show that number.

If the group of words forms a phrase, move on to the next line.

1. You can sprout almost any seed, bean, or grain

2. In a clear pint jar

3. The tastiest things to sprout

4. Sprouts are full of vitamins

5. Do you like sprouts with your salad

6. At a 45-degree angle

7. Cover the jar with cheesecloth

8. Seeds that float are sterile and will never sprout

9. Depending on the temperature

10. Does it take only 3 to 6 days to sprout seeds

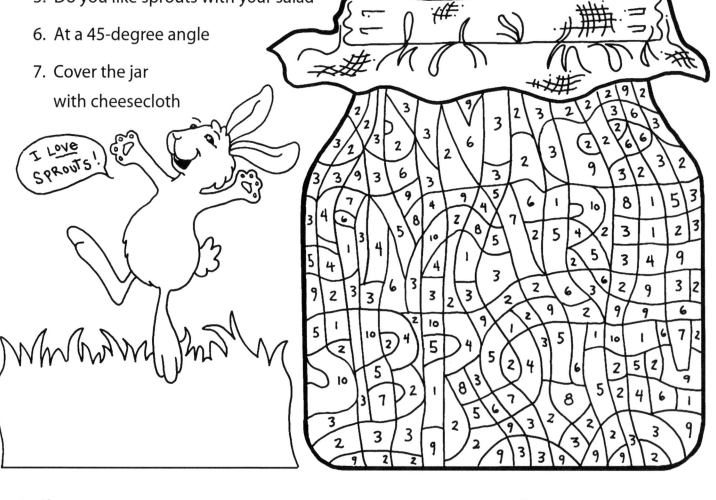

Name:

Date:

Identifying Complete Sentences

Language Literacy Lessons / Writing Intermediate
Copyright ©2002 by Incentive Publications, Inc.
Nashville, TN.

Out of this World

Write a complete sentence to tell what you would do in each of the following situations.

1. An interesting creature from another planet knocks on your bedroom window.

   _____

   _____

2. Suddenly, the lights from the spaceship start flashing.

   _____

   _____

3. The creature tells you that he has come to take you to Venus.

   _____

   _____

4. You start to get dressed and can't find your shoes.

   _____

   _____

5. As you are about to be beamed up, you realize that you forgot to leave your parents a note.

   _____

   _____

6. Up, up, and away! You are really on your way.

   _____

   _____

7. You find yourself in a room surrounded by bright lights and hundreds of large-eyed creatures.

   _____

   _____

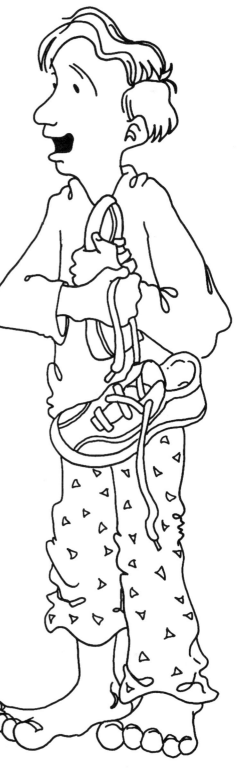

Name: _____ Date: _____

Language Literacy Lessons / Writing Intermediate
Copyright ©2002 by Incentive Publications, Inc.
Nashville, TN.

Writing Complete Sentences

EVERYBODY Has a Bad Day Once in a While

Think about a really bad day you once had.

Try to remember just exactly what happened and why it was so bad.

Write a brief paragraph telling about the events of that day.

_____

_____

_____

_____

_____

_____

_____

_____

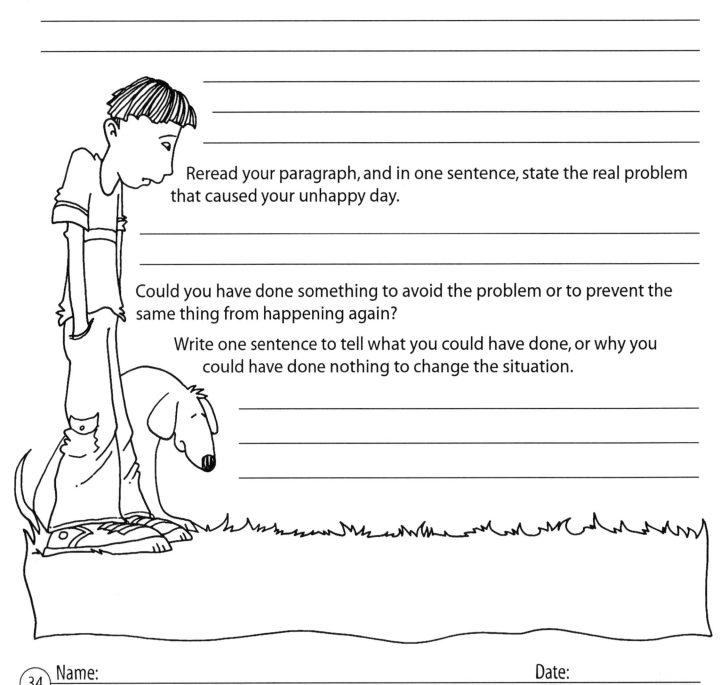

Reread your paragraph, and in one sentence, state the real problem that caused your unhappy day.

_____

_____

Could you have done something to avoid the problem or to prevent the same thing from happening again?

Write one sentence to tell what you could have done, or why you could have done nothing to change the situation.

_____

_____

_____

2 Points of View

It's amazing how differently two people can feel about the same set of circumstances.

Write the full name of one person in your class who is closest to your age.

_____

Your Date of Birth _____

Time of Birth _____

Other Person's Date of Birth _____

Time of Birth _____

In three sentences,
describe a controversial current event of interest to you and your classmates.

_____

_____

_____

Interview the person nearest your own age to get his/her point of view on the issue.

My Point of View

_____

_____

His / Her Point of View

_____

_____

Compare and contrast the two points of view.

_____

_____

_____

_____

_____

_____

Name: _____   Date: _____

Write On for Student Rights

Select one of the topics below and write a good paragraph to convince someone else that you are right.

Underline the topic sentence in the paragraph.

Don't forget to indent and to check your work for correct punctuation and capitalization.

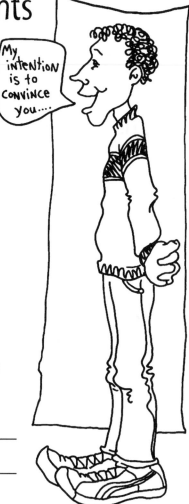

My intention is to convince you....

1. Students should be allowed to help make all school rules.

2. When accompanied by an adult, people thirteen years old and younger should be allowed to travel on airplanes and trains free of charge.

3. Teachers should never assign homework on weekends or holidays.

4. Students should be allowed to watch TV for an hour or two on school nights.

_____

_____

_____

_____

_____

_____

_____

_____

_____

_____

_____

_____

Name: _____

Date: _____

Language Literacy Lessons / Writing Intermediate
Copyright ©2002 by Incentive Publications, Inc.
Nashville, TN.

Planetary Planning

If you could visit a planet other than Earth for one day, which of these planets would you visit? Circle your choice.

Mars   Jupiter   Pluto

Use the encyclopedia to locate information about this planet.

1. Write the full name of the encyclopedia set you will be using.

   _____

2. Write the letter and the number identifying the volume in which you found the information.   Volume _____ Number _____

3. List 3 important facts about this planet and give the page number on which each fact was found.

   1. Page _____   Fact: _____

      _____

   2. Page _____   Fact: _____

      _____

   3. Page _____   Fact: _____

      _____

Use your imagination and list 3 things you might find on this planet that you could not find on Earth.

1. _____

   _____

2. _____

   _____

3. _____

   _____

Name: _____   Date: _____

Language Literacy Lessons / Writing Intermediate
Copyright ©2002 by Incentive Publications, Inc.
Nashville, TN.

Locating and Using Factual Data for Writing

Don't Panic—Plan It!

Select and circle one of the following subjects about which you would like to learn more.

Jungle animals   Space exploration   World geography

History of television   Desert plant life   Ocean farming

Number the following activities in the order in which they would be most helpful to you if you had only three days in which to prepare a class report.

____ reading library books

____ working with a group of your classmates

____ reading magazine and newspaper articles

____ studying a textbook

____ watching TV programs

____ studying with one other person

____ listening to the radio

____ using encyclopedias and other reference books

Now, write a 5-step plan for learning as much as possible about your chosen subject in three days.

1. _____

_____

2. _____

_____

3. _____

_____

4. _____

_____

_____

5. _____

_____

_____

Name: _____

Date: _____

Sequencing Ideas

Language Literacy Lessons / Writing Intermediate
Copyright ©2002 by Incentive Publications, Inc.
Nashville, TN.

Composition and Original Writing

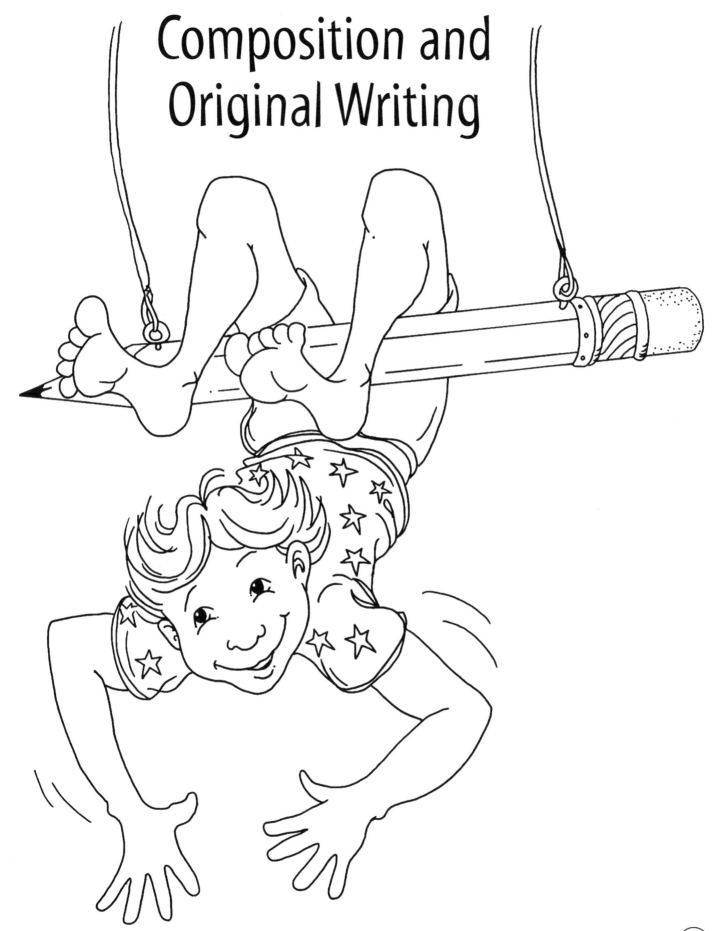

Time to Write

Professional writers say that the best way to become a good writer is to write, write, write.

Begin your writing record today.

Set a time limit for completing the record.
Keep it in your notebook until it is completed.

_____'s Writing Record

(your name)

Things to Write	Title or Comment	Date
Ad		
Autobiography		
Biography		
Cartoon		
Editorial		
Fable		
Greeting card		
Jokes		
Journal entry		
Letter		
List		
Memo		
Myth		
Note		
Novel		
Play		
Poetry		
Poster		
Recipe		
Riddles		
Slogan		
Speech		
Tall tale		

 Name: _____   Date: _____

Developing Writing Style

Language Literacy Lessons / Writing Intermediate
Copyright ©2002 by Incentive Publications, Inc.
Nashville, TN.

Step-By-Step

Choose one of the following tasks.

wrapping a birthday gift   tying a shoe   making a bed

On the lines below, write step-by-step directions for a person to follow who has never performed that task.

Number each step. After you have finished, reread your directions. Are they clear? Have you left anything out?

_____

_____

_____

_____

_____

_____

_____

_____

_____

_____

_____

_____

_____

_____

_____

_____

_____

_____

Name: _____   Date: _____

Language Literacy Lessons / Writing Intermediate
Copyright ©2002 by Incentive Publications, Inc.
Nashville, TN.

Writing Step-by-Step Directions

Making a Big Splash

This story is for you to write. Look at the pictures in all the parts.

Decide which part should begin the story. Write the words for that part. Then find the second part, and write the words for that part.

Keep going until you have finished the story. Then connect the parts in order with a squiggle line so your friends can read your story.

_____

_____

_____

_____

_____

_____

_____

_____

_____

_____

_____

_____

Name: _____

Date: _____

Sequencing Ideas

Language Literacy Lessons / Writing Intermediate
Copyright ©2002 by Incentive Publications, Inc.
Nashville, TN.

A Change of Attitude

Read the sentences below carefully.

Then build an interesting story by writing a number beside each sentence to show where it should appear in the story.

Use the lines at the bottom of the page to write a final concluding sentence to give the story a surprise ending.

_____ For that reason her black dress and Halloween hat were tattered and torn and not very presentable.

_____ So she hurriedly found a needle, thread, and some scissors.

_____ Her broomstick was getting old, and she had completely neglected to get a new sky map.

_____ The witch wardrobe catalog had not been exciting this year, and she had not ordered any new clothes.

_____ She cut and stitched, twisted and turned, and improvised in every way possible.

_____ Next she acquired a bolt of red-and-green checked gauze from her cousin for the Christmas witch.

_____ The grumpy old witch just wasn't ready for another Halloween ride.

_____ "Who ever thought of orange and black for Halloween colors anyway?" she thought. "This year I will do something different."

_____ She grabbed a star for her hat and exclaimed as she jumped on her broomstick, "It's amazing what a change of attitude can do for a grumpy witch!"

_____ Before you could say, "Trick or treat!" she had made a new hat and dress and had tied a big red bow to her broomstick.

_____ She wasn't even sure she could find her way to the village to which she was assigned.

_____ Besides all this, she was tired of the same old jack-o'-lanterns and kids' costumes and those boring candied apples and jelly beans.

_____

_____

_____

Name: _____   Date: _____

Language Literacy Lessons / Writing Intermediate
Copyright ©2002 by Incentive Publications, Inc.
Nashville, TN.

Developing Plot and Sequence

Write a Sad Story

Read the last paragraph of LuAnne's story,
and write the beginning and middle of the story.

Tell <u>why</u> and <u>how</u> poor LuAnne managed to find herself
in such a sad situation.

LuAnne saw her friends disappear around the corner. As
she looked down at her bleeding knee, her scattered books,
and her torn skirt, she thought about the events of the past
hour and began to cry. "If only I had obeyed my mother, used my
head and treated my friends a little more kindly, none of this
would have happened," she said.

Name: _____

Date: _____

Developing Plot and Sequence/Finishing a Story

Language Literacy Lessons / Writing Intermediate
Copyright ©2002 by Incentive Publications, Inc.
Nashville, TN.

Question Time

You are to be the chairman of a student group presenting a panel discussion on discipline for a school assembly. This is a very important assignment because the principal and all teachers in the school will be present.

One student from each class will be nominated as a panel participant. Since you are chairman, it is your job to interview the nominees and select the three best qualified participants.

Make a list of 7 to 10 good questions you will use to interview the participants.

1. _____

_____

2. _____

_____

3. _____

_____

4. _____

_____

5. _____

_____

6. _____

_____

7. _____

_____

8. _____

_____

Name: _____   Date: _____

Language Literacy Lessons / Writing Intermediate
Copyright ©2002 by Incentive Publications, Inc.
Nashville, TN.

Writing Interview Questions

Biographical Data

Interview an adult that you find interesting. Fill out this biographical data sheet with the information necessary to write the person's biography.

Remember, a biography must include facts, not fiction.

Name _____

Parents' names _____

Date of birth _____ Place of birth _____

Childhood *(unusual events, talents, achievements)* _____

_____

_____

Teenage years *(hobbies, academic interests, trips)* _____

_____

_____

Adult life *(occupation, special recognition, community contributions, family)*

_____

_____

Other important facts _____

_____

_____

Language Literacy Lessons / Writing Intermediate
Copyright ©2002 by Incentive Publications, Inc.
Nashville, TN.

A Life Worth Writing About

Use the information gathered on the biographical data sheet to write a biography.

A *biography* must be the true account of a person's life.

The writer can add interest by including the most exciting events, and by using colorful and creative words and sentences.

This is the biography of

_____

_____
_____
_____
_____
_____
_____
_____
_____
_____
_____
_____
_____
_____
_____
_____
_____
_____

Name: _____   Date: _____

Writing a Biography

It's Your Life

An *autobiography* is the story of a person's life, written by that person.

An autobiography includes facts about time and place of birth, family, schools attended, and places lived. A good autobiography also includes things of interest such as hobbies, friends, likes, dislikes, and dreams for the future.

Write your autobiography here.

Be sure to add some funny incidents, unique experiences, or "colorful" information. After all, you want everyone you know to be aware of how very special your life is.

_____

_____

_____

_____

_____

_____

_____

_____

_____

_____

_____

_____

_____

_____

_____

_____

_____

THE UNFORGETABLE UNBELIEVABLE AWESOME Life of ANDY MOE! WRITTEN BY ANDY MOE

Name: _____ Date: _____

Writing an Autobiography

Museum Match-Up

The pieces of this puzzle can be put together several different ways. Each way will show a different picture.

Draw the puzzle pieces in a different arrangement to form a differnt picture in the frame below.

Give your completed picture a name. Then write a brief description of it for a museum catalog.

_____

_____

_____

_____

_____

_____

_____

_____

_____

_____

_____

_____

Name: _____

Date: _____

Descriptive Writing

For Sale

Look in the classified ad section of your local newspaper for precise writing at its best. Since classified ads are paid for by the line, they are usually written with the fewest words possible.

Use the fewest words possible to write a classified ad to sell each of the items below.

Describe each item fully, and be sure to include the price and any special "selling" features.

_____

_____

_____

_____

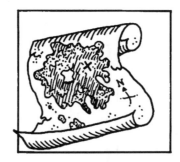

_____

_____

_____

_____

Name: _____ Date: _____

Writing Precise Descriptions

Language Literacy Lessons / Writing Intermediate
Copyright ©2002 by Incentive Publications, Inc.
Nashville, TN.

News Flash

Read the news story below carefully.

Then write five sentences to summarize this news bulletin for a radio broadcast.

Heavy winds and thundershowers began about 6:30 p.m. An hour and a half later, hurricane warnings were posted. It was about 8:30 when residents of the island knew they were in for some serious weather problems. Suddenly the lights were all out signaling that this island's electrical power was gone. This meant all phone and cable lines were down too so that communication with the outside for the time being would be impossible. By this time the waves were beating against the pier with enough force to send heavy boards and railings into the air. The wind whipped against the lighthouse and ripped off the shutters and destroyed most of the roof. Two fishing boats were overturned near the shore. Fortunately, all 6 men in the 2 boats were able to swim ashore and pull in their overturned boats. The smaller boat, however, was a total loss. One of the fishermen in this boat was knocked unconscious and was rescued by his friend, who later collapsed from exhaustion. Both men were hospitalized. Several houses were damaged severely, and a number of the island's largest trees were uprooted. This is the worst hurricane to be recorded in the island's history.

Name: _____

Date: _____

Summarizing

On the Books

Saying the same thing in a different way is called paraphrasing.

Usually paraphrasing is used to make something more clearly understood by using different words.

Paraphrase these laws made by early citizens of Wild Oats, U.S.A., to make them clearer and more concise.

Boots and heavy shoes are fine for streets and sidewalks, but should always be replaced with slippers by gentlemen entering the town hall or ballroom.

_____

_____

People who owe large sums of money for longer than ninety to one hundred sixty days and do not make payment of these debts as promised, shall be subject to a prison sentence or obligated to work for a specified number of days for the person to whom they owe money.

_____

_____

Spitting on the floor in public places is unsanitary and nasty and is prohibited by law and punishable according to the laws of the land.

_____

_____

Borrowing another person's horse or mule for your own use without first seeking permission from the owner of the horse or mule is dishonest and despicable and will be cause for a stiff fine.

_____

_____

It is not seemly or neighborly to leave a horse and buggy, or any other animal and vehicle, hitched to another person's hitching post or private property, without permission from the property owner. Any person who trespasses on another person's property in this manner will be subject to a heavy fine and confiscation of the animal and vehicle.

_____

_____

Seashore Similes

Similes are a way to compare two unlike things using the words like or as.

In the following paragraph, underline all the similes.

Complete the story by adding three sentences with similes.

    The day was as clear as a bell and as warm as a wool sweater in the winter. We were walking by the seashore and there was much to see. The seagulls were huddled on the beach like a group of people waiting to see a movie, and some of them would fly off as fast as lightning. There were small tidepools that sparkled like diamonds and had tiny crabs in them.

    At the water's edge, we saw dozens of seashells as pretty as a picture and lots of fish darting back and forth like thieves. The dune grass waved like a flag in the breeze and was surrounded by sea oats. The seashore was certainly a peaceful place—as quiet as a mouse.

_____

_____

_____

_____

_____

Name: _____

Date: _____

Language Literacy Lessons / Writing Intermediate
Copyright ©2002 by Incentive Publications, Inc.
Nashville, TN.

Recognizing and Writing Similes

What is This?

Imagine that you

- were wandering in the woods all alone on a hot summer day …
- stepped in a hole in the ground …
- felt yourself sliding on a real slide—down, down, down …
- suddenly landed on your feet in a huge, brightly lit cave!

And, as your eyes became accustomed to the glare, you saw this scene.

What in the world would you do?

How would you find out where you are and what this strange machine is?

Write 3 good questions that you would ask. Since you may use only 3, you will want to word each question very carefully.

1. _____

2. _____

3. _____

Good, Good, Good!

Teachers are always giving awards to kids. They give awards for good work, good sportsmanship, good discipline, good health habits, and other good things kids do.

Whatever it is, the kid who gets the award feels fine, because he or she knows that the teacher has seen and appreciated his or her good work.

Wonder why kids never think of giving awards to teachers?

Think of one really neat thing that your teacher does that no other teacher you know does. Describe this very special thing.

_____

_____

_____

Now, design an award for your teacher. Show your work here.

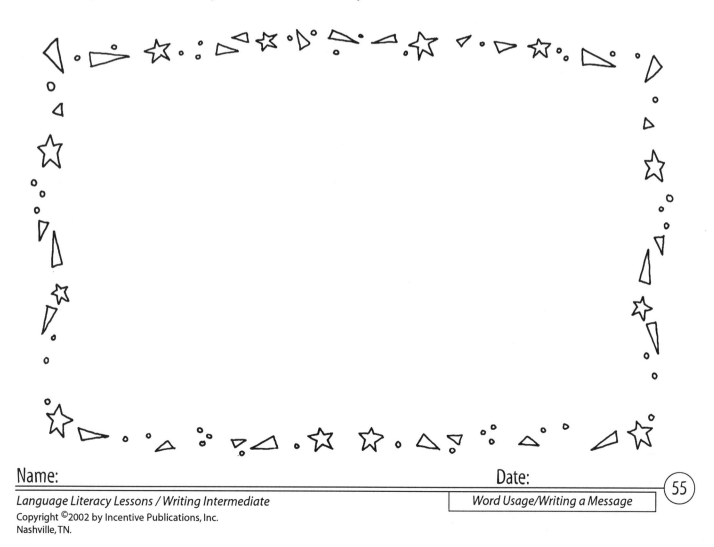

Name: _____

Date: _____

Language Literacy Lessons / Writing Intermediate
Copyright ©2002 by Incentive Publications, Inc.
Nashville, TN.

Word Usage/Writing a Message

A Letter Worth Reading

Select one of the following letters to write.

Use the most imaginative heading, greeting, body, and closing that you can.

FROM	TO
a visitor to Earth from Mars	her teacher on Mars
Cinderella	her stepmother's attorney
Mother Goose	her travel agent
the Queen of England	the President of the United States
Romeo	Juliet

Special Delivery!

Write yourself a letter of encouragement.

Begin by stating the problem that bothers you most right now. Tell what you think caused the problem and how it developed. Then, tell what you think you can do about it, and express confidence in your ability to solve the problem. Try to make this letter honest, but say what you want to hear, too.

☆ FROM: Me!
☆ To: Myself!

_____
_____
_____
_____
_____
_____
_____
_____
_____
_____
_____
_____
_____
_____
_____
_____
_____
_____

♡ Me

When you finish your letter, reread it to see if your problem sounds as big as you thought. Fold your letter, put it in your notebook and don't look at it again for a week.

At the end of the week, take it out, read it and decide if the letter helped you solve your problem.

Name: _____

Date: _____

Writing a Letter (Introspective Writing)

Uninvited Picnic Guests

Write the conversation that is taking place.

Then draw a panel to show what will happen next.

Name:

Date:

Writing Conversation

Script Writer

Choose one of the following stories to rewrite as a television series.

Divide the story and make a plan for presenting this story in 3 parts.

Write the dialogue on another sheet of paper.

"Jack and the Beanstalk"
"Cinderella"
"Hansel and Gretel"

Story _____

Characters _____

_____

Plot and plan for Part I _____

_____

_____

_____

_____

Plot and plan for Part II _____

_____

_____

_____

_____

Plot and plan for Part III _____

_____

_____

_____

_____

Name: _____ Date: _____

Language Literacy Lessons / Writing Intermediate
Copyright ©2002 by Incentive Publications, Inc.
Nashville, TN.

Writing Dialogue

Tell-Tale Bags

Sometimes you can tell a lot about a person by the things she or he carries around. What do these bags tell you about their owners?

Study each bag and its contents carefully. Draw a portrait in each frame to show how you think the owner looks.

Write a description of each owner (age, sex, personality, height, weight, etc.) on the lines provided in each picture.

60 Name:
Characterizing/Writing Sentences

Date:

Language Literacy Lessons / Writing Intermediate
Copyright ©2002 by Incentive Publications, Inc.
Nashville, TN.

An Air of Mystery

Name the mystery character and complete her identification card.

Give her a destination and an assignment.

Write the story of her trip.

Identification Card

Name _____

Address _____

_____

Age _____ Color of eyes _____

Height _____ Weight _____

Occupation _____

Destination _____

Assignment _____

_____

_____

_____

_____

Story

_____

_____

_____

_____

_____

_____

_____

_____

Name: Date:

Language Literacy Lessons / Writing Intermediate
Copyright ©2002 by Incentive Publications, Inc.
Nashville, TN.

Characterizing/Writing Sentences

On Stage

Spread your hand wide open and draw around your fingers.

Add features, clothing, and any other details to make each of the 5 fingers into a make-believe character.

On another sheet of paper, write a play featuring the 5 characters.

Be sure that your play has an interesting title, setting, plot, and climax.

Name:

Date:

Writing a Play

Language Literacy Lessons / Writing Intermediate
Copyright ©2002 by Incentive Publications, Inc.
Nashville, TN.

Comical Characters

Write a silly consonant story to fit each comical character. In each story, use as many words as possible that begin with the same letter as the character's name.

Patchwork Pete

Patchwork Pete from Pittsburgh puts peanuts in pans and pails. He likes pumpkin pie, pineapple, and popcorn. He punches people who poke at pigs! Pete wears pink pantaloons, drives a purple pickup, and plays piccolo in the band.

Ragged Rex

Jamie Jumper

Tilly Toad

Careless Carolyn

Beautiful Betsy

Wealthy William

Name: _____   Date: _____

Language Literacy Lessons / Writing Intermediate
Copyright ©2002 by Incentive Publications, Inc.
Nashville, TN.

Writing Nonsense Stories

The Travels of Tracy and Tony

Tell a tall tale about the travels of Tracy and Tony.

Use as many *T* words in the story as you can.

T words

(Use your dictionary to find more.)

try	train	told	through	trod	took
trip	tense	trend	trust	tread	take
travelogue	twilight	teacher	trick	thorough	toward
tiny	thirsty	trembled	track	throw	traffic
tremendous	Thursday	triumphant	trail	truck	turn

Tracy and Tony were terrified as they traveled timidly down the tiny tree-lined trail.

_____

_____

_____

_____

_____

_____

_____

_____

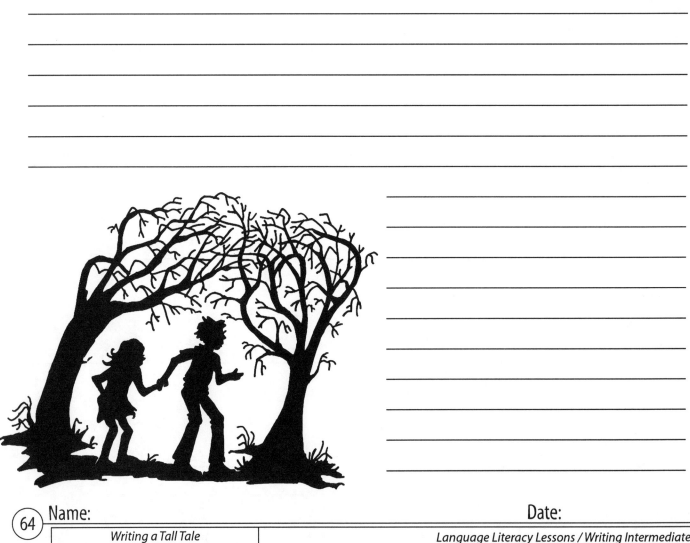

_____

_____

_____

_____

_____

_____

_____

_____

_____

Writing a Tall Tale

Write Your Story

Select one of these titles for the picture below:

An Upside-Down Day   A Funny Forest   An Animal Mix-Up

Write your title on the line provided.

_____

Use the same title for the picture but make it much more exciting.

Look carefully again at the picture.

Draw at least three more items in the picture to better reflect the title selected.

Then write the story to go with your title and illustration. Use the back of this sheet to complete your story.

_____

_____

_____

_____

Name: _____   Date: _____

Language Literacy Lessons / Writing Intermediate

Copyright ©2002 by Incentive Publications, Inc.
Nashville, TN.

Developing Visual Imagery

Kaleidoscope

Use your colored markers to make this beautiful kaleidoscope even more beautiful.

Try to use every marker you have at least once.

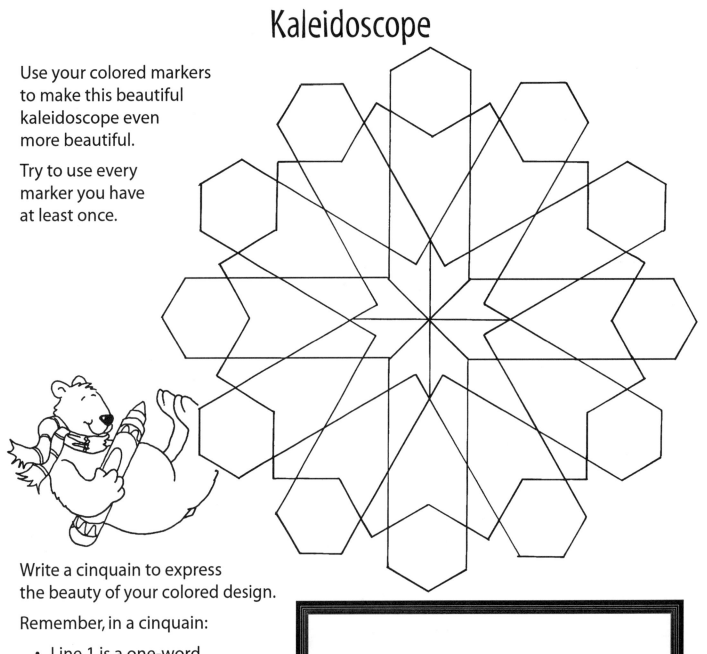

Write a cinquain to express the beauty of your colored design.

Remember, in a cinquain:

- Line 1 is a one-word subject or idea.

- Line 2 is two adjectives describing the subject.

- Line 3 is three verbs showing action related to the subject.

- Line 4 is four words giving your personal reaction to the subject.

- Line 5 is a one-word synonym for the subject.

Name:

Date:

Writing a Cinquain

Language Literacy Lessons / Writing Intermediate
Copyright ©2002 by Incentive Publications, Inc.
Nashville, TN.

You're a Poet, and You Know It!

To write an acrostic, write the word which is the theme of the poem vertically down the left-hand side of the paper.

Each line across begins with the letter that is at the beginning of the line.

Use the letters in your own name to write an acrostic in the frame below.

Decorate the frame, cut it out, and use it for a bookmark.

Pull your thoughts together
On anything you choose;
Employ your sense of rhythm,
Make your words amuse!

A Laugh a Day

Have you thought about laughter as a good health habit? A laugh a day can help people stay healthy, and sometimes, laughter helps sick people get well.

Write a complete sentence to finish the "laughs" below.

Then, finish the "Laugh-A-Day" calendar on the following page. Write a corny joke, a riddle, a knock-knock, a cartoon, a tongue twister, or whatever it takes to tickle your funny bone in each of the seven spaces. Add fun illustrations, and give your finished calendar to someone who needs a good laugh. *(Note: mailing it with a "your secret pal who wishes you a good laugh" signature will make it even more fun for your special person.)*

KNOCK, KNOCK.

Who's there?

Otter.

Otter who?

You Otter

_____

_____

_____

Looks like:

_____

_____

_____

What did the Papa Screech Owl say to the baby Screech Owl on the way to the skating rink?

_____

_____

_____

Why did the lone motorcycle rider use only back roads?

_____

_____

_____

Name: _____

Writing Jokes

Date: _____

Language Literacy Lessons / Writing Intermediate
Copyright ©2002 by Incentive Publications, Inc.
Nashville, TN.

Laugh-A-Day Calendar

Write or draw a joke for every day of the week.

SUNDAY

MONDAY

TUESDAY

WEDNESDAY

THURSDAY

FRIDAY

SATURDAY

HA-HA!

GRIN!

Hee!

YUK-YUK!

HA!

CHUCKLE!

HO!

Name:

Date:

Writing to Express Humor

Captions Count

Write two good cartoon captions for this picture.

What are the implications of each caption you have written?

Decide which one is more creative. Use the caption you selected as the starter for a brief creative story. Write the story on the back of this sheet.

Compare the thoughts conveyed by the caption and the story.

Which is more interesting?

Why?

Caption 1: _____

Caption 2: _____

Name: _____ Date: _____

Writing Captions for a Story/Critiquing Own Writing

Language Literacy Lessons / Writing Intermediate
Copyright ©2002 by Incentive Publications, Inc.
Nashville, TN.

Way to Go

Make each of the shapes below into a vehicle to take you to another planet.

Then complete the information box for each vehicle.

On the back of this sheet, write an imaginative story to tell about your planetary journey.

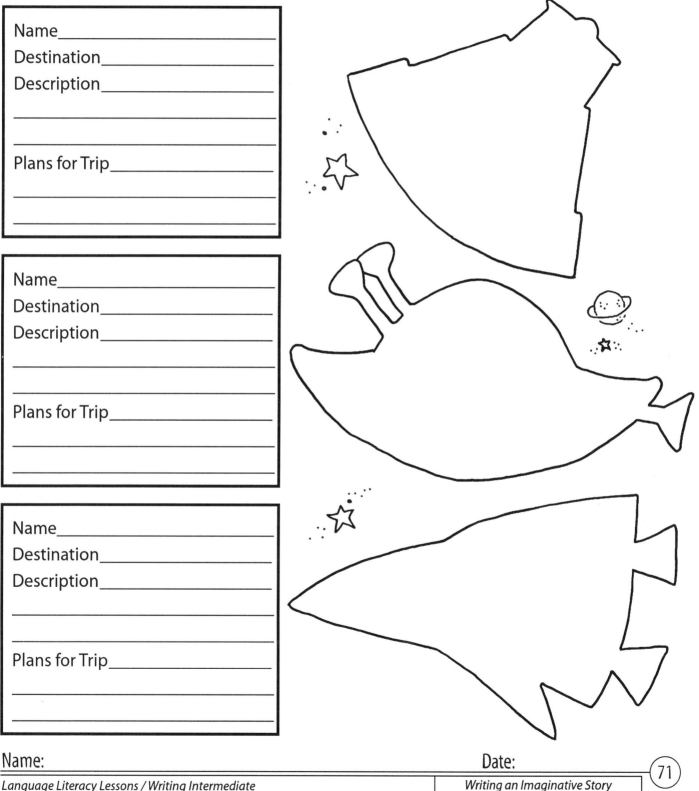

Name_____

Destination_____

Description_____

_____

_____

Plans for Trip_____

_____

_____

Name_____

Destination_____

Description_____

_____

_____

Plans for Trip_____

_____

_____

Name_____

Destination_____

Description_____

_____

_____

Plans for Trip_____

_____

_____

Name: Date:

Language Literacy Lessons / Writing Intermediate

Copyright ©2002 by Incentive Publications, Inc.
Nashville, TN.

Writing an Imaginative Story

What Would Have Happened?

Write three good sentences to tell what would have happened if …

1. …Isabella, the Queen of Spain, had refused to finance Columbus's voyage to the New World.

_____

_____

_____

2. …all the barnyard animals had worked together to help the Little Red Hen bake bread.

_____

_____

_____

3. …The school board in your town had voted last year to close all the schools in the system for three years.

_____

_____

_____

4. …the printing press had never been invented.

_____

_____

_____

5. …cars, trucks, and buses had been banned from all interstates fifteen years ago.

_____

_____

_____

Name: _____

Date: _____

Developing Original Ideas

Language Literacy Lessons / Writing Intermediate
Copyright ©2002 by Incentive Publications, Inc.
Nashville, TN.

Good Luck

Write a sentence to tell what you think about when you see a picture of a four-leaf clover.

_____

_____

Then finish the story below.

Good Luck for Mario

Mario couldn't believe all the things that had happened today. This had certainly been a day he would never forget. He blew his nose, dried his tears, and smiled.

And now, right there in front of him, was the first four leaf clover he had ever seen. Then he picked the four-leaf clover and sat down to think about how his luck had changed. The day had started . . .

Name: _____ Date: _____ 73

Finishing a Story/Imaginative Writing

No Happy Ending in Sight

Read the unfinished story
below. Then, write an ending to make it a very bad day, indeed, for poor George.

As George took his brand new ice skates from the box, he was thinking about the wonderful time he would have skating on the ice-covered pond in the park around the corner. He rushed to the phone to call and ask his friend Josef to meet him at the pond. Josef's mother answered the phone and told George that Josef was in bed with the mumps. She reminded George that he and Josef had been together every day for the past two weeks, including yesterday when Josef was beginning to complain about being hot and having a very sore throat. She said that since George had most certainly been exposed to the mumps, maybe he should stay home today.

George's throat did feel strange, and when he opened the door to let his dog out, the cold air made it feel worse. He was so anxious to try his new skates, however, that he decided to go on to the park. In his haste, he forgot his gloves and he couldn't remember where he had left his hat and muffler the night before.

He ran all the way to the park because he wanted to be on the ice before the other kids arrived. When he got there, he noticed a sign at the pond's edge, but he just didn't take the time to stop and read it. His head was hurting and he really felt hot and out of breath when he got to the pond, but he hastily strapped on his skates and rushed onto the ice.

_____

_____

_____

_____

The View from Below

Dolphins sometimes offer rides to people, and seem to take delight in sharing games with humans. There also have been many cases of dolphins helping humans in difficult situations, taking care not to hurt them. The dolphin family (called Cetaceans) has a high level of intelligence, and some think this may be a reason for the caring attitude.

Pretend you are swimming in the ocean and a dolphin offers you a ride; take a deep breath and hang on to the dorsal fin. It won't be easy to breathe at the fast speed that the dolphin travels, but you will most likely have an exciting ride!

Write a story of the ride from the dolphin's point of view.

_____

_____

_____

_____

_____

_____

_____

_____

_____

_____

_____

_____

_____

_____

_____

_____

_____

_____

Name: _____   Date: _____

Language Literacy Lessons / Writing Intermediate
Copyright ©2002 by Incentive Publications, Inc.
Nashville, TN.

Writing an Imaginative Story

The Last Story

Pretend that you are holding the last pencil in the world.

Think carefully before writing your story.

Then write what could be the world's last story.

THE LAST PENCIL IN THE WORLD

_____

_____

_____

_____

_____

_____

_____

_____

_____

_____

_____

Name:

Date:

Writing an Imaginative Story

Language Literacy Lessons / Writing Intermediate

A Matter of Perspective

Writing from a different perspective is a fun way to exercise your imagination and to learn to express yourself more creatively. Shel Silverstein, a famous poet whose work you have no doubt enjoyed, created a poem in which he pretended he was writing from inside a lion. Now that was a different perspective!

Try your hand at writing from an unusual perspective by writing a mini-story from both of these unusual environments. Don't forget that even a mini-story includes who, what, when, and where.

Inside a suitcase, on the conveyor belt at the airport.

_____

_____

_____

_____

_____

_____

_____

Inside a spacecraft, just before "blast off."

_____

_____

_____

_____

_____

_____

_____

_____

Name: _____   Date: _____

The End

Good writers know that strong endings are very important for stories, reports, letters, advertisements, and in almost all creative writing.

If the reader is left with a weak ending, the lasting impression is probably going to be that the whole piece is representative of weak writing skills.

Develop your skills as a strong writer by supplying good endings that might be used for one of the writing examples below.

1. A vicious and damaging storm that occurred in a neighboring town last night

2. A report of a major theft at a local jewelry store

3. A plea for preservation of a community landmark scheduled to be demolished to make way for a high-rise office building

_____

_____

_____

_____

_____

_____

_____

_____

Date:

Answer Key

Page 13

lounging, studying, passed, walking, talking, called, waved, bask, worry, thinking, review, eat, shining, study, opened, spread, selected, gave, completed, fell

Page 14

big, giant, huge, best-liked, favorite, large, oversized, clear, crystal, glass, sweet, sugary, syrupy, billowy, fluffy, whipped, little, small, chopped, luscious, bright, red, delicious-looking, scrumptious-tasting

Page 15

1. frequently
2. positively
3. approximately
4. partially
5. eagerly
6. apparently
7. soon
8. barely
9. precisely
10. remarkably

Page 17

Once there was a very <u>handsome</u> <u>prince</u>. He was <u>tall</u> and <u>fair</u> and had <u>long</u>, <u>blond</u>, <u>curly</u> hair. His clothes were of the <u>finest</u> <u>white</u> <u>silk</u>, and his <u>new</u> <u>boots</u> were made of <u>leather</u> and were <u>carefully</u> sewn together. His hand was <u>strong</u>, and he often used his <u>sparkling</u> <u>sword</u> to do <u>good</u> deeds. He was very <u>happy</u>, for everyone <u>loved</u> him. People <u>enjoyed</u> him because of his <u>pleasant</u> nature. He always had <u>kind</u> things to say, and tried to <u>help</u> people in trouble.

Page 18

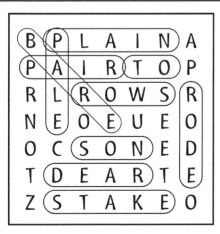

Page 25

What would you do if you found yourself on a strange planet and the only sign of life you saw was a rock that had "Punctuation Planet" written on it? Maybe you would look for a trail or footprints. I don't know what I would do, but one thing I do know is that I would be frightened. I would want to find a friend or two or look for a way to send a message back to Earth. I would begin to look around for food, shelter, and clothing just in case no rescue came. Can you imagine being in this punctuation situation?

Page 26

king's throne
queen's crown
princess's cloak

dog's fleas
beggar's rags
watchman's keys

Page 27

A fox fell into a well and was unable to escape. He was trying to solve his problem when a thirsty goat came along.

The goat asked, "Is the water good and do you have enough?"

The fox replied, "There is plenty of delicious water, please come and quench your thirst."

The goat couldn't resist and leaped into the well. The fox climbed up on the goat's horns and escaped.

When he got out, he called down to the trapped goat and said, "If you had half as much of a brain as you have a beard, you would have looked before you leaped."

Page 29

Peter awoke suddenly and sat up in bed. He held his hand over his mouth to smother the scream that he felt was coming. His heart beat wildly and he could hardly breathe! Where was that strange noise coming from? The same "thud, thud, thud," then a loud "clump," was repeated over and over. It sounded like a large body coming downstairs 3 at a time, resting on the fourth step, and starting over. Peter knew, however, that there were no steps inside the house. As he crept silently from his bed, he thought to himself, "Why, oh, why did I insist on staying home alone on Friday the thirteenth?"

311 Center Street
Plaintown, Kentucky
Thursday, August 2

Dear Jerry,

This has been a long, hot summer. I have been busy with several projects. Last Tuesday, July 31, was my birthday. Karen gave me a book entitled The Runaway Princess. It was written by a famous author named Gloria T. Whipple, who lives in Santa Ana, California. I heard that she was born in Denmark and that she speaks French, English, and Dutch. Mr. Thompson, our English teacher, told me about her early life.

I hope you will be coming to Plaintown soon.

Yours Truly,

Barbara Ann

My cousin Becky came to visit for the first time. I wanted to give her the grand tour of my neighborhood so she could meet all my friends. We walked up and down the block and I introduced her to some people. I said that we would all play together after dinner. Then, I took out some of my allowance. I said I would treat Becky to an ice cream cone, but she preferred a Popsicle instead. We arrived home in time for dinner, but neither of us was hungry. We stared at our food. We sat for an hour. We couldn't eat, but all the other kids were back outside. They were choosing teams for a kickball game. We were wishing that we had waited until after dinner for dessert. But, it was too late to worry about a decision we had made in haste and without thinking about the consequences. It looked as if another day might pass before Becky got to play with my friends.

6, 8, 2, 5, 10, 9, 1, 7, 12, 11, 3, 4

The day was as clear as a bell and as warm as a wool sweater in the winter. We were walking by the seashore and there was much to see. The seagulls were huddled on the beach like a group of people waiting to see a movie, and some of them would fly off as fast as lightning. There were small tidepools that sparkled like diamonds and had tiny crabs in them.

At the water's edge, we saw dozens of seashells as pretty as a picture and lots of fish darting back and forth like thieves. The dune grass waved like a flag in the breeze and was surrounded by sea oats. The seashore was certainly a peaceful place—as quiet as a mouse.